Let's DRAW!

DOGS

How2DrawAnimals

Walter Foster
Jr.

Brimming with creative inspiration, how-to projects, and useful information to enrich your everyday life, quarto.com is a favorite destination for those pursuing their interests and passions.

© 2022 Quarto Publishing Group USA Inc.
Illustrations and text © 2022 P. Mendoza

First published in 2022 by Walter Foster Jr., an imprint of The Quarto Group.
100 Cummings Center, Suite 265D, Beverly, MA 01915, USA.
T (978) 282-9590 F (978) 283-2742 www.quarto.com • www.walterfoster.com

Walter Foster Jr. titles are also available at discount for retail, wholesale, promotional, and bulk purchase. For details, contact the Special Sales Manager by email at specialsales@quarto.com or by mail at The Quarto Group, Attn: Special Sales Manager, 100 Cummings Center, Suite 265D, Beverly, MA 01915, USA.

ISBN: 978-0-7603-8072-7

Digital edition published in 2022
eISBN: 978-0-7603-8073-4

Printed in China
10 9 8 7 6 5 4 3

TABLE OF CONTENTS

TOOLS & MATERIALS

Welcome! You don't need much to start learning how to draw. Anyone can draw with just a pencil and piece of scrap paper, but if you want to get more serious about your art, additional artist's supplies are available.

PAPER If you choose printer paper, buy a premium paper that is thick enough and bright. Portable sketch pads keep all your drawings in one place, which is convenient. For more detailed art pieces, use a fine art paper.

PENCILS Standard No. 2 pencils and mechanical pencils are great to start with and inexpensive. Pencils with different graphite grades can be very helpful when shading because a specific grade (such as 4H, 2B, or HB) will only get so dark.

PENCIL SHARPENER Electric sharpeners are faster than manual ones, but they also wear down pencils faster. It's most economical to use an automatic one for inexpensive pencils and a manual sharpener for expensive ones.

ERASERS Some erasers can smear, bend, and even tear your paper, so get a good one that erases cleanly without smudges. Kneaded erasers are pliable and can be molded for precise erasing. They leave no residue, and they last a long time.

PENS If you want to outline a drawing after sketching it, you can use a regular Sharpie® pen or marker. For more intricate pieces, try Micron® pens, which come in a variety of tip thicknesses.

DRAWING BASICS

How to Draw Shapes

For the first steps of each project in this book, you will be drawing basic shapes as guide lines. Use light, smooth strokes and don't press down too hard with your pencil. If you sketch lightly at first, it will be easier to erase if you make a mistake.

You'll be drawing a lot of circles, which many beginning artists find difficult to create. These circles do not have to be perfect because they are just guides, but if you want to practice making better circles, try the four-marks method, as shown below.

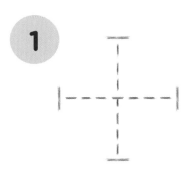

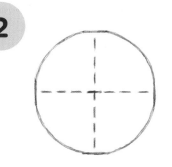

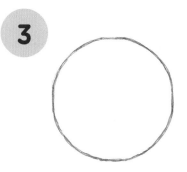

1 Mark where you want the top of the circle and, directly below, make another mark for the bottom. Do the same for the sides of the circle. If it helps, lightly draw a dotted line to help you place the other mark.

2 Once you have the four marks spaced apart equally, connect them using curved lines.

3 Erase any dotted lines you created, and you have a circle!

ADDITIONAL SHAPES While circles are usually what people find the most challenging, there are many other lines and shapes that you should practice and master. An arc can become a muzzle or tongue. Triangles can be ears, teeth, or claws. A football shape can become an eye. A curvy line can make a tail and an angled line a leg. Study the animal and note the shapes that stand out to you.

How to Shade

The final step to drawing an animal is to add shading so that it looks three-dimensional, and then adding texture so that it looks furry, feathery, smooth, or scaly. To introduce yourself to shading, follow the steps below.

1

Understand your pencil with a value scale. Using any pencil, start to shade lightly on one side and gradually darken your strokes toward the other side. This value scale will show you how light and dark your pencil can be.

2

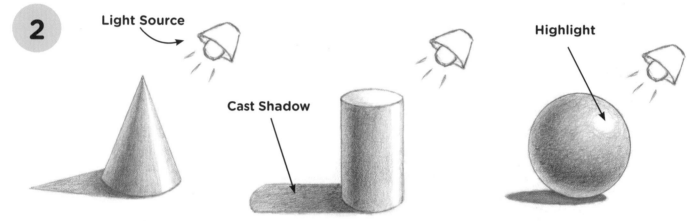

Light Source

Cast Shadow

Highlight

Apply the value scale to simple shapes. Draw simple shapes and shade them to make them look three-dimensional. Observe shadows in real life. Study how the light interacts with simple objects and creates shadows. Then try drawing what you see.

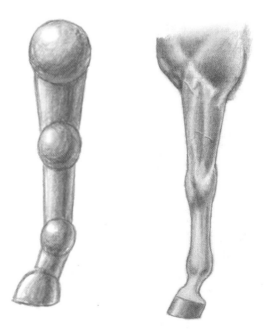

3

Practice with more complex objects. Once you're comfortable shading simple objects, move on to more complex ones. Note, for example, how a horse's leg is made up of cylinders and spheres. Breaking down your subject into simple shapes makes it easier to visualize the shadows.

How to Add Texture

Take what you've learned about shading one step further by adding texture to your drawings.

FURRY

One quick pencil stroke creates a single hair. Keep adding more quick, short strokes and you'll get a furry texture. Separate each individual stroke a bit so that the white of the paper comes through.

Create stripes and patterns by varying the pressure on your pencil to get different degrees of tonal value.

Make sure that your strokes follow the forms of the animal. As you shade a furry animal, use strokes that go in the general direction of the fur growth. The fur here follows the form of a simple sphere.

 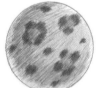

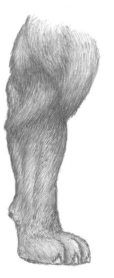

This is how to add fur to a complex form, which is easier if you know the animal's anatomy. In order to show the muscle structure, this image shows an exaggerated example of a lion's front leg and paw.

SMOOTH

For very short fur or smooth skin, add graphite evenly. Blend with a cotton swab, blending stump, or piece of tissue if needed.

SCALY

For scaly animals like reptiles or dragons, create each individual scale with a tiny arc. Then add shadows to make the form look three-dimensional.

For a much easier way to get a scaly look, just add a bunch of squiggles! Make the squiggles darker in areas of pattern, as well as when adding shadows.

FEATHERED When adding texture to feathered animals, approach it as you would with fur or with smooth skin. Use a series of short strokes for fine or fluffy feathers. For smooth feathers, use even, blended value.

GERMAN SHEPHERD

1

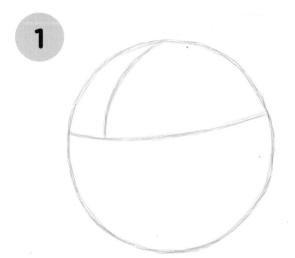

Draw a big circle as a guide for the German Shepherd's head. Then add a long, curved, horizontal line across the circle and a curved, vertical line on the top, left side. These lines will help you place the facial features later.

2

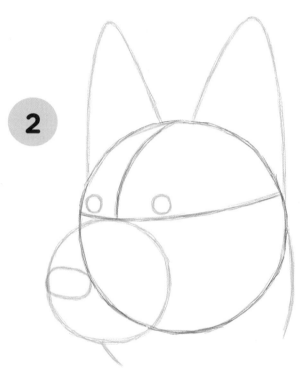

Draw a circle as a guide for the muzzle and add a small oval inside for the nose. Add two circles as guides for eyes and triangles for ears. Also draw a couple of curved lines for an indication of the dog's neck.

3

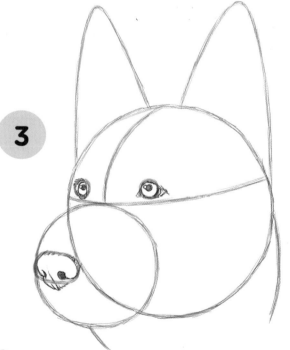

DRAWING THE EYE When drawing the eye, include a tiny circle to represent a highlight on the eyeball. Then draw a slightly larger circle for the pupil and shade it in, being careful not to overlap the highlight circle.

Lightly sketch the eyes inside the head. The eye on the left should be a bit thinner than the eye on the right because the dog's head is slightly turned. Then lightly sketch the nose. Once you get the lines just right, darken them.

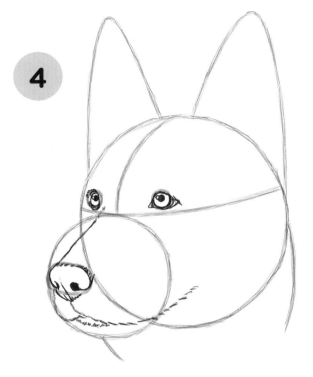

4 Draw the lines for the muzzle lightly at first. When you get them right, darken them using short strokes for the fur.

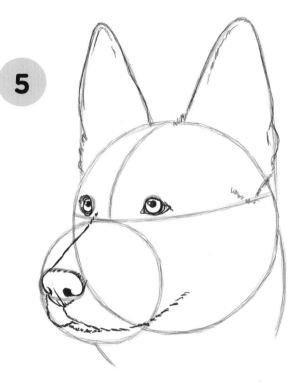

5 Darken the arcs on the top of the head to create the ears, adding a few curves and details.

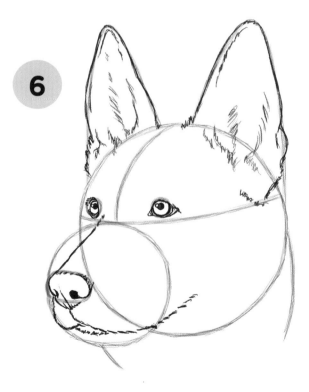

6 Add a series of short strokes in the ears for the inner ear structure and for the fur found there.

7 Use quick, short pencil strokes along the path of the original head circle to create the furry shape of the head. Note where the line follows the original guides and where it deviates from them.

8

Add more details in the head, such as short strokes above the eyes for the brow and along the neck for skin folds.

9

For a cleaner look, erase as much as you can of the initial guide lines. Don't worry about erasing all of the guides. It's okay to leave some behind. Redraw any final sketch lines you may have accidentally erased.

10

Shade your German Shepherd for extra detail. Study the image carefully, noting the areas of the lightest, darkest, and middle values. See where your pencil strokes should be short and quick for short fur, while other areas should have longer, lighter strokes, such as in the ears. Other areas will have smooth shading, such as in the eyes and on the nose.

SHADING Remember that shading can take a very long time to complete, so be patient and take breaks. Slowly build up the value by adding more and more strokes until you're happy with the result, and make sure to use pencil strokes that go in the general direction of the fur. It also requires a lot of practice to be able to shade well, so you may want to make a copy of your final sketch so you can try several times.

CORGI

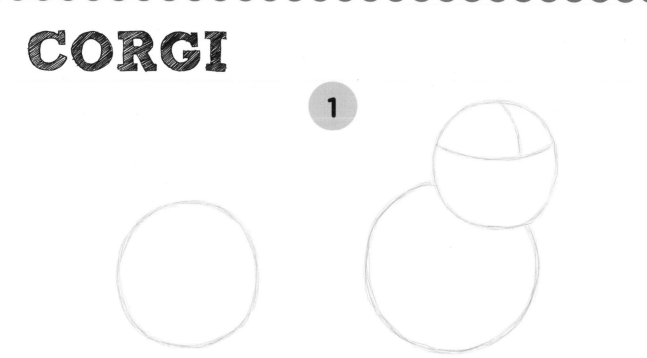

Lightly sketch three circles on your page. Note their sizes and placement, and how the guide for the head overlaps one of the body circles. Include two curved lines in the head, which will help you place the facial features later.

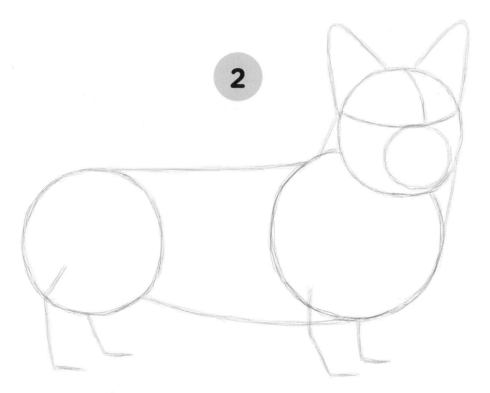

Finish up your guide lines by drawing a small circle for the muzzle, triangles for the ears, lines to complete the neck and body, and four angled lines for legs. Corgis have very short legs, so these guide lines should be short as well.

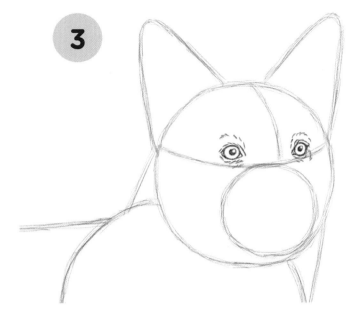

3

Lightly sketch the eyes, and when you get the placement of the eyes right, darken them. The eye on the right side should be a tiny bit smaller because of the perspective. Make sure to include the highlights and pupils inside the eyes, and lines around the eye for detail.

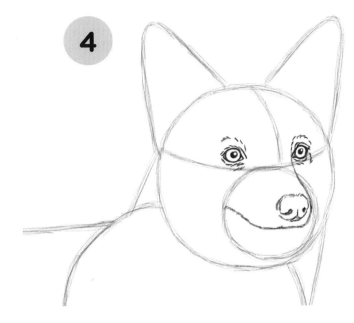

4

Draw the nose by first lightly sketching a small oval, and then darkening the small details, including the dark nostrils, detail lines, and furry strokes on top of the nose. Then add the top part of the muzzle as a curved line made up of furry strokes.

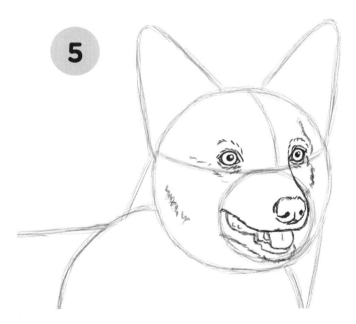

5

The open mouth shows the tongue and gums, in addition to the furry chin. Pay attention to all the small details of the mouth as you draw it. Add some furry spots within the face for detail.

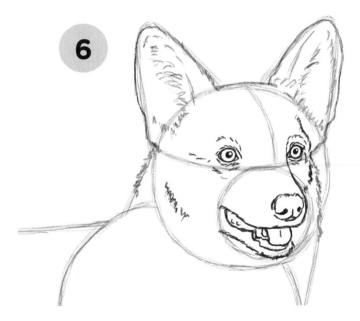

6

Use the triangles on the head as guides to draw the large ears, using quick, short strokes inside for additional fur. Then use the main circle as a guide finish up the head.

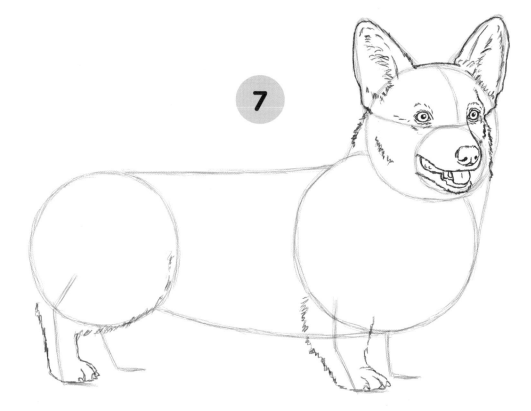

7

Use the leg guides to lightly sketch the two short, stubby legs that are most visible to the viewer. When you get the basic shape of the leg right, darken the lines using quick, short strokes. Add toes and nails on the paws.

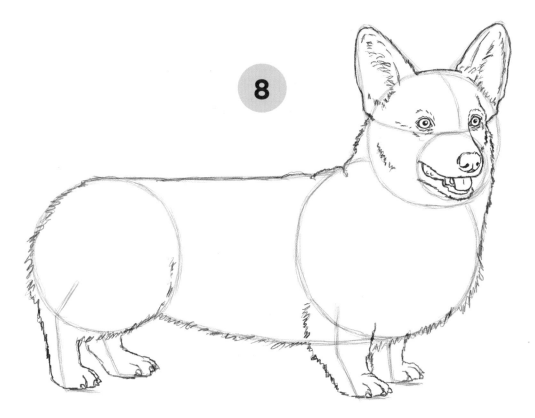

8

Finish the body shape, using longer strokes on the underside of the body for the longer fur found there. Then, using the first two legs that you drew as templates, complete the visible portions of the other two legs.

For a cleaner look, erase as much as you can of the initial guide lines. Then re-draw any final sketch lines you may have accidentally erased.

9

First add some shadows to give your dog more dimension and volume, making sure not to forget the cast shadow underneath. Then add the typical Pembroke Welsh Corgi coat pattern using a light-to-medium value that's slightly lighter than the shadows. Draw a line under the eyes and up the forehead and shade everything above this line. The muzzle should be white. Cover the rest of the body with the light-to-medium value as well, except for the chest, underside, and legs. Remember to use strokes that go in the general direction of the fur!

10

GOLDEN RETRIEVER

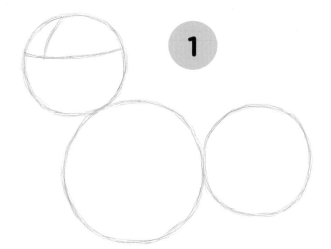

1

Draw three circles as guides for the body and head. Inside the head circle, draw two curved lines that will help you place the dog's facial features later.

2

Draw a guide for a tail and four legs coming from the body circles. Bend the leg lines where the joints and feet will be.

3

Finish up the guide lines with a big circle for the muzzle, angled lines for the floppy ears, and lines connecting the body and head circles.

4

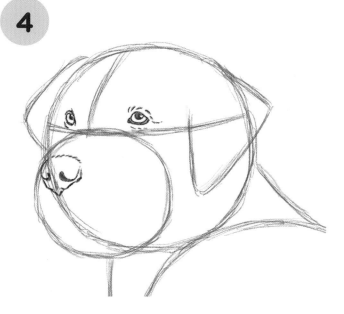

Carefully add the eyes inside the head using the construction lines as guides for placement. Include a few lines around the eyes for detail, and then sketch the nose. Note the different shapes of the nostrils, the short strokes on the top edge of the nose, and the V shape for the very bottom of the nose.

5

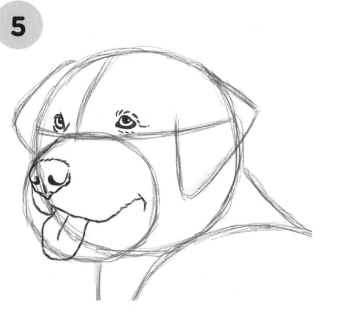

Now draw the muzzle and tongue hanging out of the dog's mouth. The tongue should stretch toward the outside of the initial circle. Add a line in the middle for extra detail.

6

Add the inside of the mouth by first drawing a small triangle-like shape for the canine tooth. For the gums and lip, add long wavy lines that meet the top lip on the right. Then draw the head and ears, following the basic paths of the original guides but using quick, short strokes to represent fur.

7

Add the final fur details in the Golden Retriever's head using quick, short pencil strokes.

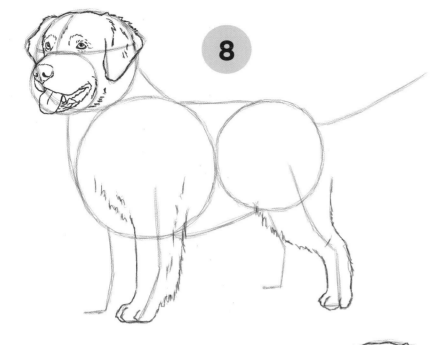

8

Use lines under the body as guides to draw the first two legs. Follow the path of the guides and draw the legs around them, using smooth lines on the front and longer strokes for furry parts. Add a couple of small, curved lines at the tip of each foot to separate the toes.

9

Using the first two legs as templates, draw what's visible of the legs on the other side.

10

Use the remaining lines as guides to draw the rest of the body. Longer strokes along the underside show that the fur there is longer. For the top part of the body, simply darken the outer edges of the initial guides.

11

Tidy up your sketch, erasing the initial guide lines and re-drawing anything you'd like to fix.

Golden Retrievers don't have any pattern on their coats like spots or patches, so just add a medium value to the whole body. Use shorter strokes when you add the value to the head as opposed to the longer strokes you will use for the body. Use a dark value on the nose, eyes, and mouth. Add some shadowed areas and a cast shadow underneath.

12

FUR TEXTURE The strokes on the Golden Retriever's chest should have a vertical orientation, while on the back and tail, the strokes should be horizontal. As you add the value, separate each individual stroke a bit so that the white of the paper comes through and creates a furry-looking texture.

HUSKY PUPPY

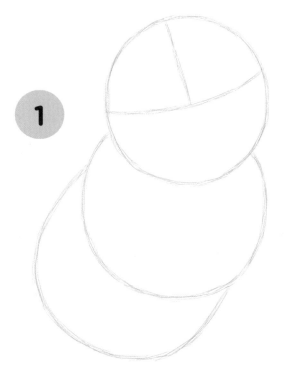

1 Lightly sketch your guide lines, beginning with three overlapping shapes and two guide lines in the head.

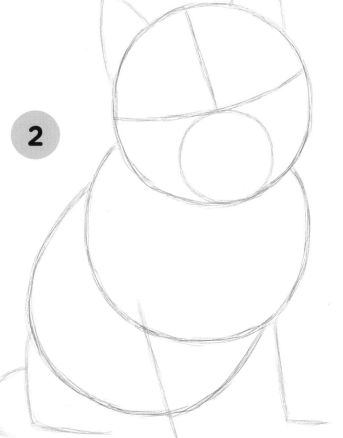

2 After adding guides for the muzzle, ears, legs, and tail, you have completed the guide lines for this drawing and can move on to adding the details!

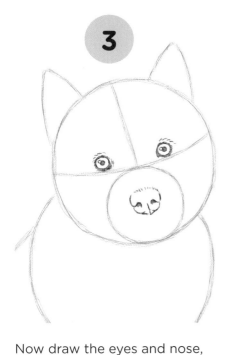

3

Now draw the eyes and nose, using the shapes from the first two steps to place them correctly on the head. Take your time, as these features have a lot of small details.

4

Use quick, short pencil strokes to create the mouth and ears.

5

Finish the head, making the sides wider as you follow the basic path of the initial circle. Use quick, short strokes to give the head a furry texture.

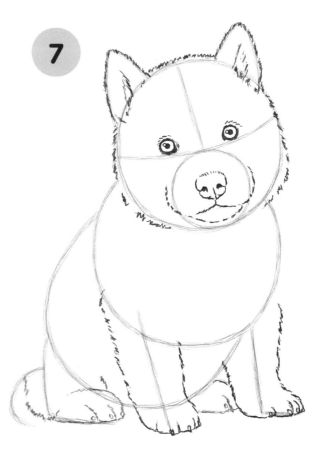

6

Draw the front legs, again using quick, short strokes to convey their furriness. The shape of the legs and feet should be short and wide, with lines at the bottom for the toes and nails.

7

Use the angled guide line under the body to draw the first hind leg. Then with a few curved lines, draw the other hind leg peeking between the body and front foot.

8

Use the remaining lines as guides to draw the rest of the body and tail. Again, use quick, short strokes to create a furry texture. Add some more strokes above the hind foot for the furry underside.

9

Stop here for a sketch or clean up your drawing to get it ready for shading.

10

Add some shadows to give the puppy more dimension and volume, with a bit of shading underneath so it won't appear to be floating. For the pattern, first draw a thin strip on the forehead between the eyes and a shape over each eye, which you will leave white. As you add value, use strokes that go in the general direction of the fur and don't shade too smoothly. On the head, the strokes should radiate outward. The lower half of the head should be white, and the nose should have the darkest value. Add some value to the left side of the body as well, leaving the chest and underside white.

BEAGLE

Start this drawing with three circles for guides. Make sure to note their sizes and relation to one another.

Add two lines in the head circle, which will help you place the facial features later on. Then sketch some lines and shapes for leg guides at the bottom.

After adding guides for the muzzle and ears, neck and body, and tail, you have completed the guide lines for this drawing and can move on to adding the details!

1

2

3

4

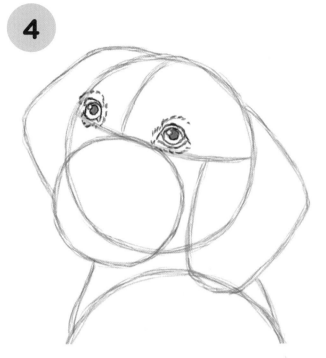

Now draw the eyes, using the guide lines to place them correctly on the head. Take your time adding the highlight circles and pupils, the smooth lines around the eyes, and furry strokes for additional detail. Note how the eye on the left looks smaller because of the way the head is turned.

5

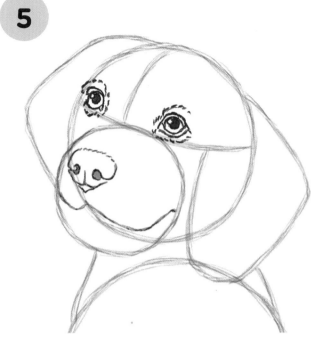

Draw the nose and top part of the mouth and muzzle, paying attention to all the details in the nose.

6

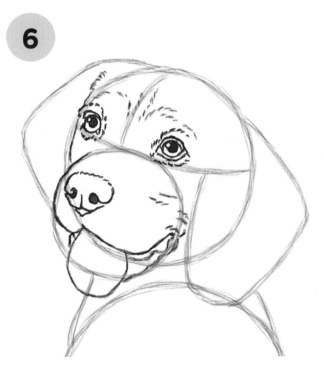

Add the tongue and wavy lip. Draw some of the head on the left by the eye. Then use quick, short pencil strokes for detail throughout the face, including the brow area.

7

Finish the head, which is flat on the top, and add the large, floppy ears with wavy lines and quick, short pencil strokes.

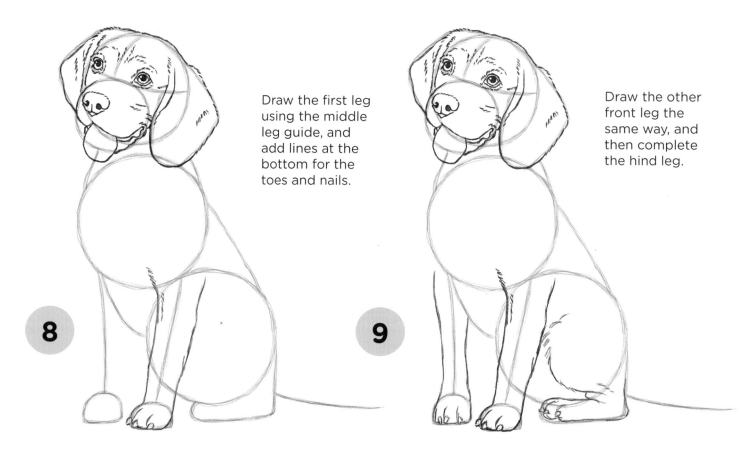

Draw the first leg using the middle leg guide, and add lines at the bottom for the toes and nails.

8

Draw the other front leg the same way, and then complete the hind leg.

9

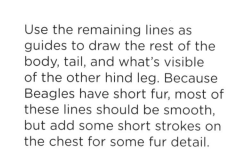

10

Use the remaining lines as guides to draw the rest of the body, tail, and what's visible of the other hind leg. Because Beagles have short fur, most of these lines should be smooth, but add some short strokes on the chest for some fur detail.

Stop here for a sketch or clean up your drawing to get it ready for shading.

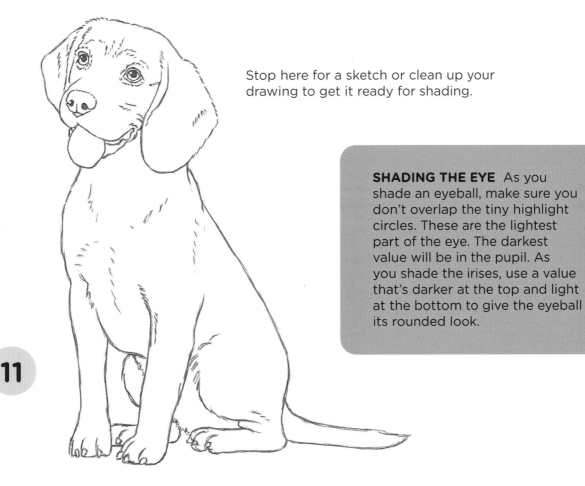

SHADING THE EYE As you shade an eyeball, make sure you don't overlap the tiny highlight circles. These are the lightest part of the eye. The darkest value will be in the pupil. As you shade the irises, use a value that's darker at the top and light at the bottom to give the eyeball its rounded look.

11

First add some shadows to give the dog more dimension and volume, with a bit of shading underneath so it won't look like it's floating. For the pattern, first draw a thin strip on the forehead between the eyes, which you will leave white. Shade in the direction of the fur growth and shade a little more smoothly because of the short fur. The lower part of the head and the underside of the body should be white, and the nose and back should have a darker value.

12

BOSTON TERRIER

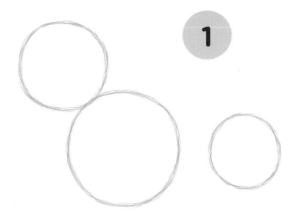

1

Start with three circles for the body and head. Pay attention to their sizes and placement in relation to each other.

Connect the circles with lines, and add two slightly curved lines to the head circle. These lines in the head will help you know where to draw the facial features later on.

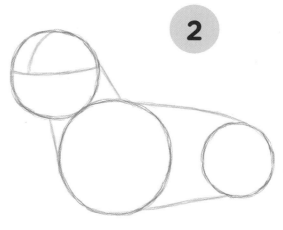

2

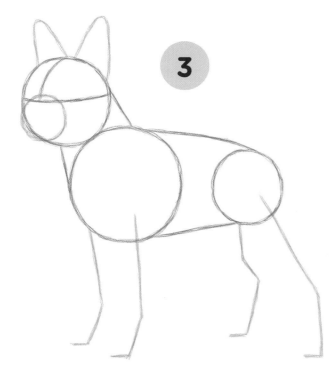

3

After you add a circle for the muzzle, triangular arcs for the ears, and lines for the legs and feet, you have completed the guide lines! Note that the leg lines will bend at the joints and where the feet will be.

SHORT FUR Because Boston Terriers have short fur, don't use quick, short pencil strokes for fur. Instead, use wavy or curved lines. This gives the dog a smoother appearance, not a shaggy one. Boston Terriers are easy to shade because you don't have to worry about creating the fur texture. Simply shade smoothly over the area.

4

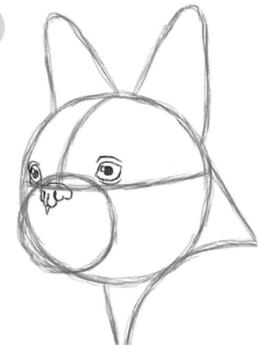

Carefully sketch the eyes and nose using the initial lines as guides for placement. Draw lightly at first and darken the shapes only when you get their sizes and positions to your liking. Note how the eye on the left is smaller because of the angle of the dog's head.

5

Draw wavy lines under and around the nose for the mouth and muzzle.

6

Darken the arcs on the head for the ears, adding a few extra lines for the inner structure of the ear. Then use the big initial circle as a guide to draw the rest of the head. Note that on the left side, the wavy line is closer to the eye to make the shape of the head narrower than the original circle. Also draw a short, curved line over each eye to emphasize the thick brows.

7

Add a few more short lines within the head and ears to give everything more structure and detail.

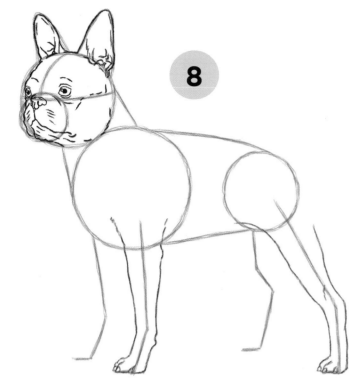

8

Draw the first two legs by following the paths of the guides and lightly sketching the legs around them. The tops of the legs should be wide and the bottoms narrow. Bend the leg to indicate the joints, and at the bottom, draw a couple of curved lines with small, triangular shapes on the tips for the toes and nails.

Now draw the legs on the other side of the body. Don't forget the toes and nails at the bottom.

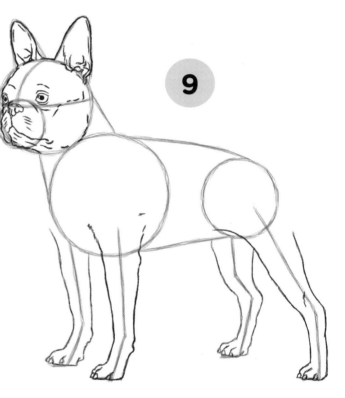

9

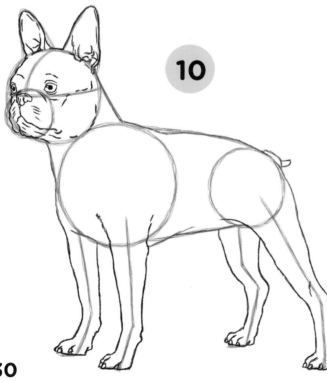

10

Use the remaining lines and shapes as guides to draw the rest of the Boston Terrier's smooth body. Curve the line at the line at the bottom for the chest, and make sure not to overlap the legs on this side of the body as you finish. On the top, right side of the body, draw the curly tail.

11

For a cleaner look, erase any extra lines, and then tidy up your sketch.

12

Outline the areas that will separate the classic black-and-white markings. Then use a dark value and smooth shading to create the black markings on the body. Using a light value, add some shadows to the white areas of the body to give the figure more volume. Then add a cast shadow underneath to finish your drawing.

GERMAN SHORT-HAIRED POINTER

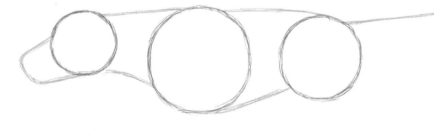

Draw three circles as guides for the head and body. Note each circle's size and placement in relation to each other.

1

On the lower, left side of the head circle, draw an arc as a guide for the muzzle. Connect all the circles with lines, and use a line to add the tail on the right.

2

Using lines, add the guide for the ear, as well as the legs. Note the angled line that serves as a guide for the dog's lifted front foot. The shape of this guide line should be similar to a big, tilted letter Z. Pay attention to how the rest of the leg guides bend.

3

4

Draw the eye, lightly at first, adding the pupil, highlight, eyelid, brow, and other detail lines. Then sketch the nose at the tip of the muzzle, darkening the lines when you are happy with their placement. Finally, follow the path of the ear guide, but make the lines curvier as you, darken them. Inside the shape, draw a few curved lines for extra detail on the folds of skin.

5

Draw the muzzle and head using the initial line and shapes as guides. Note the wavy line for the lip and curve at the brow.

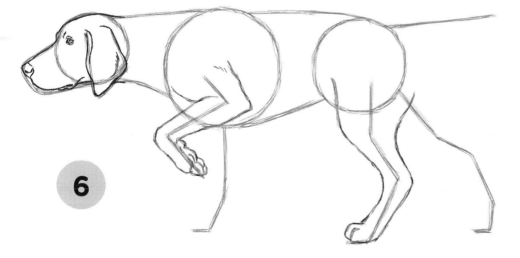

Use the angled Z-shaped line under the body as a guide to draw the front leg. At the bottom, draw the big paw facing up using a series of curved lines. Then draw the hind leg the same way but with the paw facing down. The legs should be wide at the top and gradually become thinner near the feet.

6

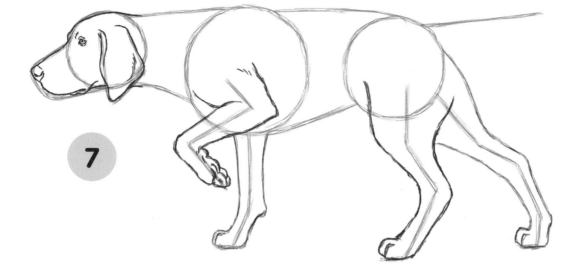

7

Draw the other two legs using the initial lines as guides. Bend the legs at the joints and add curved lines on the paws for toes.

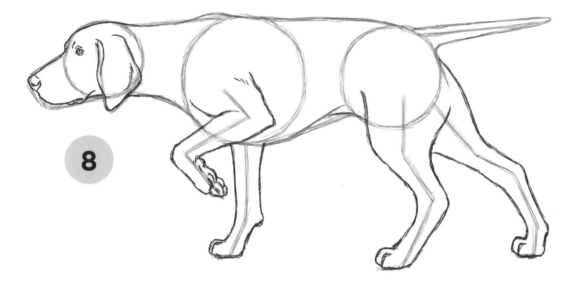

8

Use the remaining lines and shapes as guides to draw the rest of the Pointer's body. Note where the lines curve out and in. Make sure to curve the bottom up and in for a thinner stomach. Then use the line at the top as a guide to draw the pointy tail.

YOUR OWN PATTERN Feel free to copy this final step exactly or create a different coat pattern! If you have a pet Pointer, take a photo for reference and include its pattern on your drawing.

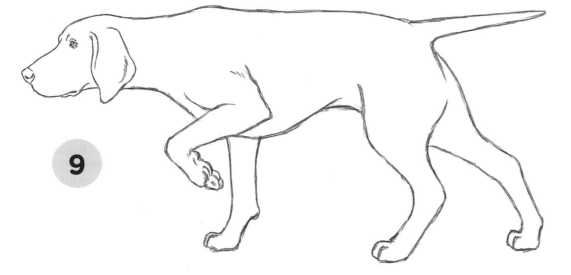

9

Tidy up your drawing by erasing guide lines and fixing any details that you'd like.

10

Add some shading to give the dog dimension and volume, and add a cast shadow on the ground underneath it. Either stop here for a white Pointer or add spots for a typical English Pointer pattern. Shade around the eye and on the ear using a medium value. For the pattern on the body, simply draw large random shapes and smaller dots and shade them in with a medium value. Continue to darken the shadows to emphasize the muscle structure until you're happy with the result.

BULLDOG

With light, smooth pencil strokes, draw a big circle as a guide for the Bulldog's head. Add two curved lines, one horizontal and one vertical, as guides that will help you place the facial features.

1

Now draw basic shapes and lines for the muzzle, nose, eyes, and ears. Note how the eye on the left will partially be hidden by the muzzle.

2

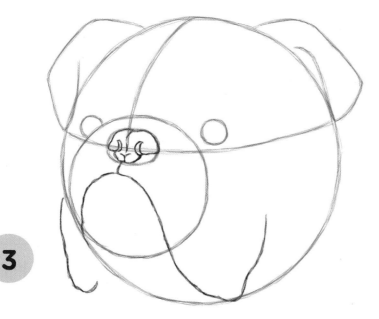

Use the small oval inside the muzzle as a guide to draw the nose using a series of small lines and curves. Below the nose, draw a big, curved line for the first part of the mouth and jowls. Add another curve just outside of the circle for the other side of the jowls.

3

Draw the skin fold on top of the nose and finish the loose skin on the chin with wavy lines. Add some short lines below the nose and on the chin for all the small wrinkles.

4

Now add the eyes. Draw a curved line across the top of each eye and curved lines on the bottom so they look droopy. Add the eyeballs inside, complete with pupil and highlight circles. Finally, add short strokes above the eyes for the brows.

5

Follow the paths of the ear guides, but make the shapes curvier as you darken the lines. Add a few longer lines for the inner structure of the ears and a series of short pencil strokes for the furry bases.

6

Use the big circle as a guide to draw the rest of the head, paying close attention to how the line curves. Draw a few curved lines to the right of the jowls for a bit of structure on the jaw, and add a bit of loose skin on the neck.

7

Draw a series of short strokes and curved lines within the shape for more detail, including more of the brows, bone structure, and loose skin on the head. These curved lines also give the Bulldog more expression and character.

8

For a cleaner look, erase as much as you can of the initial guides. Then re-draw any final sketch lines you may have accidentally erased.

9

Use a medium value to add some shadows to give the head more dimension and volume. Use a darker value in certain areas like inside the ears for deeper shadows. Shade the nose and eyes, but leave some light areas for shiny highlights. Add value to give the Bulldog its coat pattern. Finally, add a bit of light value on the white fur.

10

ALASKAN MALAMUTE

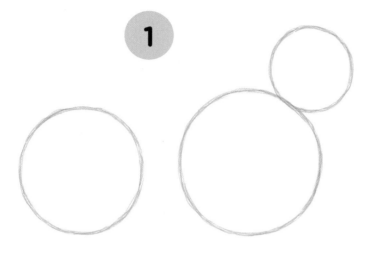

1

Draw three circles for guides, paying attention to their sizes and placement in relation to each other. Don't draw the circles too far apart or the dog's body and neck will be too long.

2

Add in guides for the muzzle, ears, body and neck, legs, and curved tail.

3

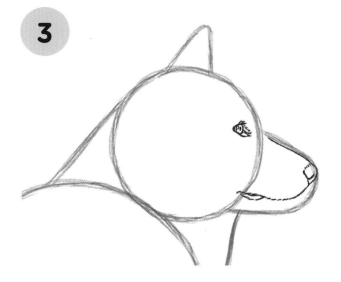

The dog is facing to the side, so only draw one eye. Sketch lightly at first, and darken the lines when you are ready. There are a lot of little details! Then add the nose, muzzle, and part of the lip.

4

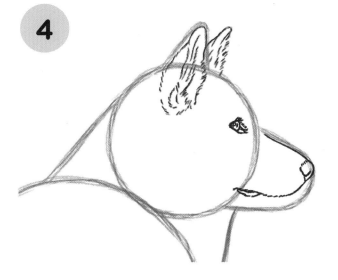

Create the first ear, making it extend lower into the head and adding a curved line at the bottom for the base. Draw a series of strokes within the shape for the fur. To the right, draw a smaller, thinner triangular shape for the other ear, and add strokes for fur.

5

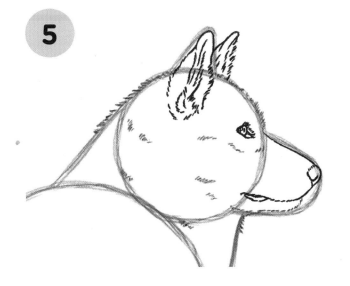

Now draw the rest of the head using a series of short strokes along the top of the head, chin, and neck. Then add short strokes inside the head for extra detail on the fur.

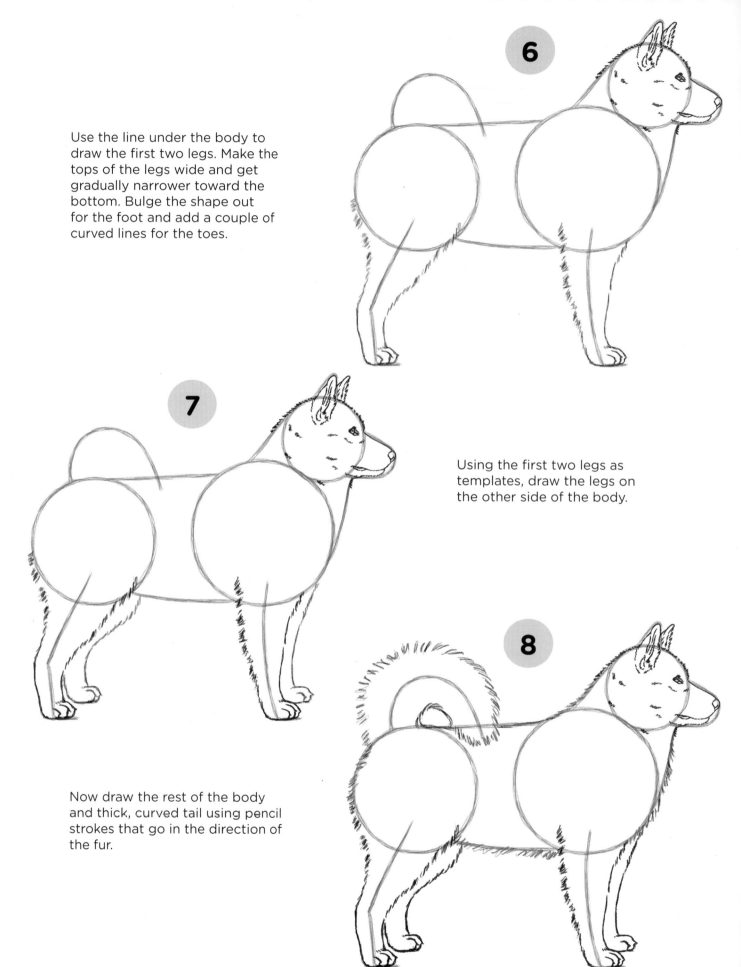

Use the line under the body to draw the first two legs. Make the tops of the legs wide and get gradually narrower toward the bottom. Bulge the shape out for the foot and add a couple of curved lines for the toes.

6

7

Using the first two legs as templates, draw the legs on the other side of the body.

8

Now draw the rest of the body and thick, curved tail using pencil strokes that go in the direction of the fur.

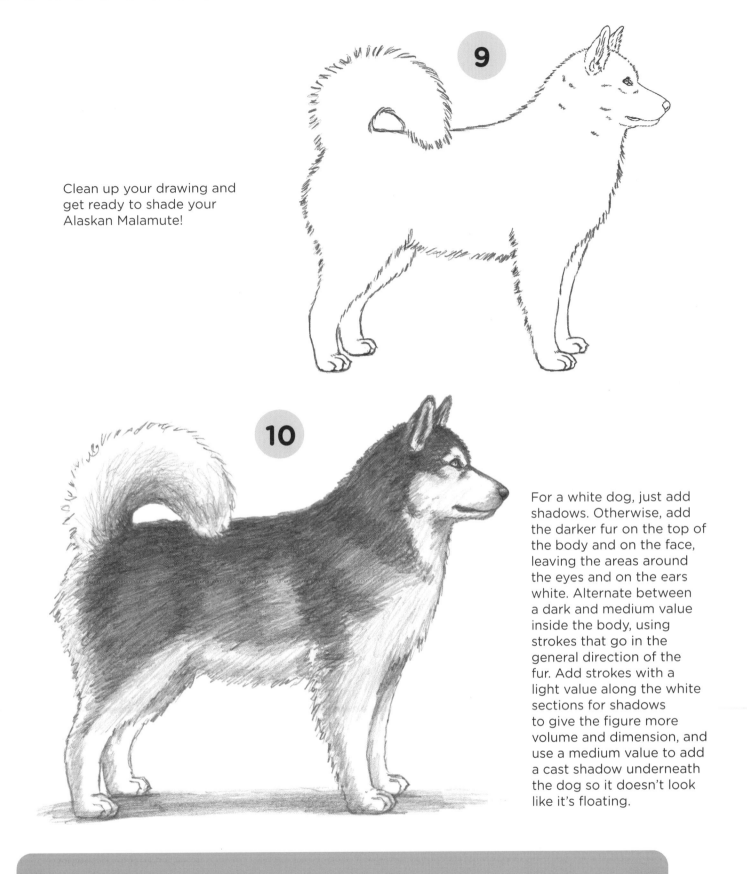

9

Clean up your drawing and get ready to shade your Alaskan Malamute!

10

For a white dog, just add shadows. Otherwise, add the darker fur on the top of the body and on the face, leaving the areas around the eyes and on the ears white. Alternate between a dark and medium value inside the body, using strokes that go in the general direction of the fur. Add strokes with a light value along the white sections for shadows to give the figure more volume and dimension, and use a medium value to add a cast shadow underneath the dog so it doesn't look like it's floating.

DIMENSION & VOLUME To make a drawing look three-dimensional, decide where the light source should be coming from and create shadows where they should appear. It helps to study shadows in real life using photo references and observing the world around you. When drawing animals, it helps to know your subject's anatomy, including the muscles underneath the fur you're drawing.

POODLE

1 Begin by lightly sketching three circles as guides for the body and head. The middle circle is a lot bigger because it's a guide for the big, puffy chest.

2 On the head circle, draw a small arc for the muzzle and a long, curved line on top of the head, which stretches back down to the big body circle. Add four lines under the body as guides for the legs. Draw yet another circle on the top, right side as a guide for the puffy tail.

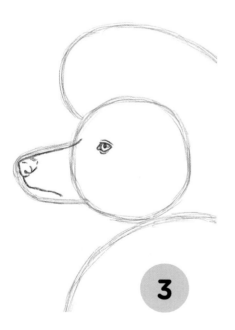

3 Take your time drawing the eye and nose, sketching lightly at first. Then add the top part of the muzzle and mouth.

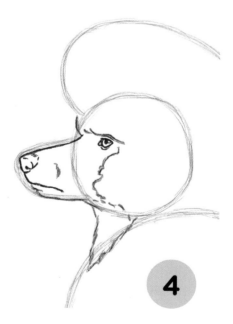

4 Draw the chin and jaw. Then add the puffy hair that outlines the face and neck.

5

Use the curved line above the head as a guide to draw the fluffy hair found there. Follow the path of the guide but use short, curved lines as you darken the shape.

6

Draw the ear, which is similar to a rectangle. The actual ears are smaller, and most of this shape is long hair. Add a few wavy lines within the shape and a line on the left side for the visible part of the other ear.

7

Use the initial circle on the left side as a guide to draw the fluffy hair on the chest. Use short, curved lines as you follow the basic path of the circle, but make the shape wider.

8

Use the lines under the body as guides to draw two of the legs. Add an oval at the bottom for the hair found there. Create toes and nails on the feet.

9

Now draw the legs on the other side using the first legs as templates.

Complete the body with two more puffs of hair on the hips and one big puff on the tail. Finish the tail and rump with smooth lines.

10

11

Clean up your drawing to get it ready for shading.

12

Add dimension and volume with some shading, and don't forget the cast shadow underneath. This is a white Poodle with light skin, so leave the hair white. Then add a medium value to the skin and a dark value to the eyes and nose. Poodles can have different-colored coats as well as darker skin, so you can add more value for a different coat and skin color.

ABOUT THE AUTHOR

How2DrawAnimals.com teaches beginning artists how to draw all kinds of animals from A to Z through video demonstrations and simple step-by-step instructions. Started in 2012 by an animal-loving artist with a bachelor's degree in illustration, How2DrawAnimals offers a new tutorial each week and now boasts hundreds of animal drawing tutorials. Working in graphite and in colored pencils, and in both realistic and cartoon styles, How2DrawAnimals has featured animals from all letters of the alphabet, from Aardvark to Zebra and everything in between. See more at How2DrawAnimals.com.

ALSO IN THE LET'S DRAW SERIES:

Let's Draw Cats
ISBN: 978-0-7603-8070-3

Let's Draw Favorite Animals
ISBN: 978-0-7603-8074-1

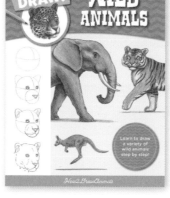

Let's Draw Wild Animals
ISBN: 978-0-7603-8076-5

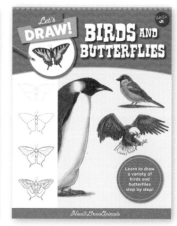

Let's Draw Birds & Butterflies
ISBN: 978-0-7603-8078-9

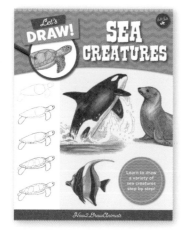

Let's Draw Sea Creatures
ISBN: 978-0-7603-8080-2

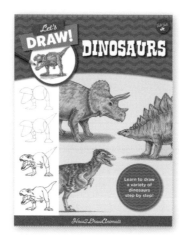

Let's Draw Dinosaurs
ISBN: 978-0-7603-8082-6

Let's Draw Dragons
ISBN: 978-0-7603-8084-0

Inspiring | Educating | Creating | Entertaining

www.WalterFoster.com